# The CURE

The Ambiguity of Love

Published by 73 Homage
ISBN# 978-0-578-83695-9

73 Homage LLC
www.73homage.com
Instagram: @73homage

*Dedicated to my*
*"what if"*

# PREFACE

**The Cure** is a story of love vs. lust when two strangers cross paths at "The Harlem"— an upscale jazz club. Lightnin' Hopkins, a 25-year-old architect and local poet known for his sensual and romantic poetry, and Paris Lawson, a 36-year-old no-nonsense successful doctor who puts her work at the forefront, cross paths one fate filled night in search of "**the cure**."

# A-SIDE: ETERNITY

A Story Of Love told from the point of view of Lightnin' Hopkins. Although Hopkins comes off as a bit of a ladies' man, he yearns for true love. Hopkins is performing at "The Harlem" when he sees the woman of his dreams walk in (Paris Lawson). As he tries to woo her with his words, he knows she has the cure to his woes.

MY LOVE ISN'T FOR EVERYONE, BUT MY LOVE GAME IS STRONG

I WON'T FORCE MY LOVE ON YOU THOUGH

IF YOU DON'T WANT MY LOVE I'LL WALK AWAY

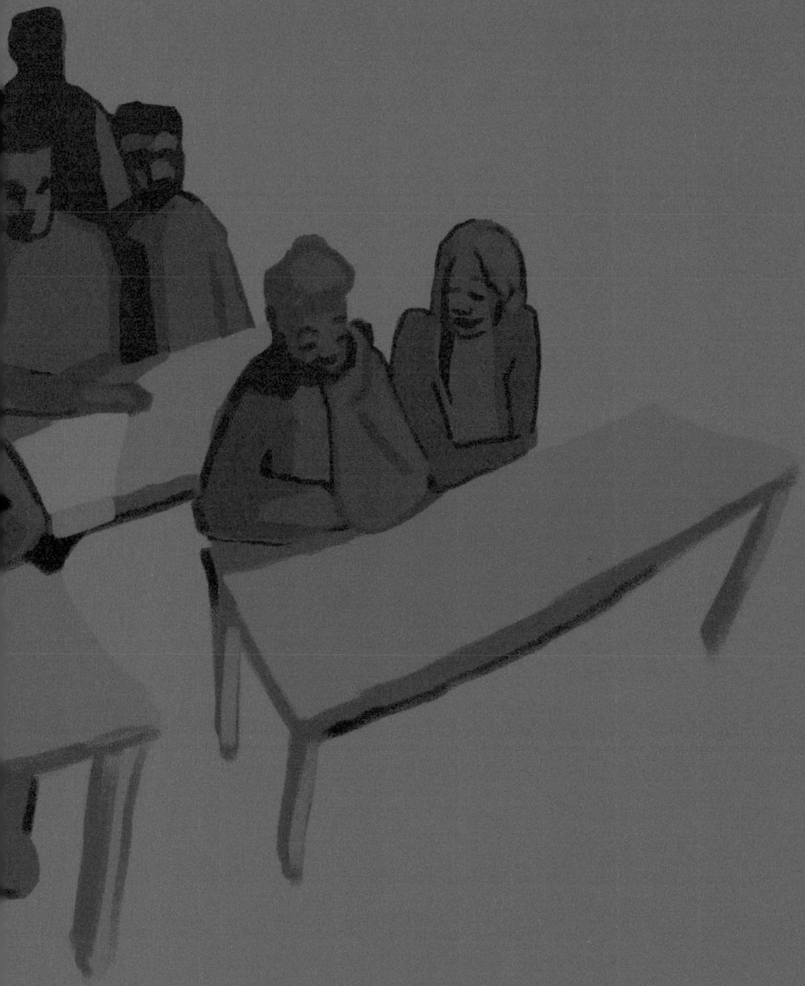

BUT THIS IS A ONCE IN A LIFETIME TYPE OF LOVE,

THE TYPE OF LOVE YOU PRAY ABOUT

THE TYPE OF LOVE THAT WILL HAVE YOU FALL DEEPER THAN YOU'VE EVER FELL

THE TYPE OF LOVE YOU'VE ONLY SEEN IN MOVIES

THE TYPE OF LOVE THAT WILL HAVE YOU FORGET ABOUT YOUR EXs

THE TYPE OF LOVE THAT WILL MAKE YOU WEAK AT THE KNEES

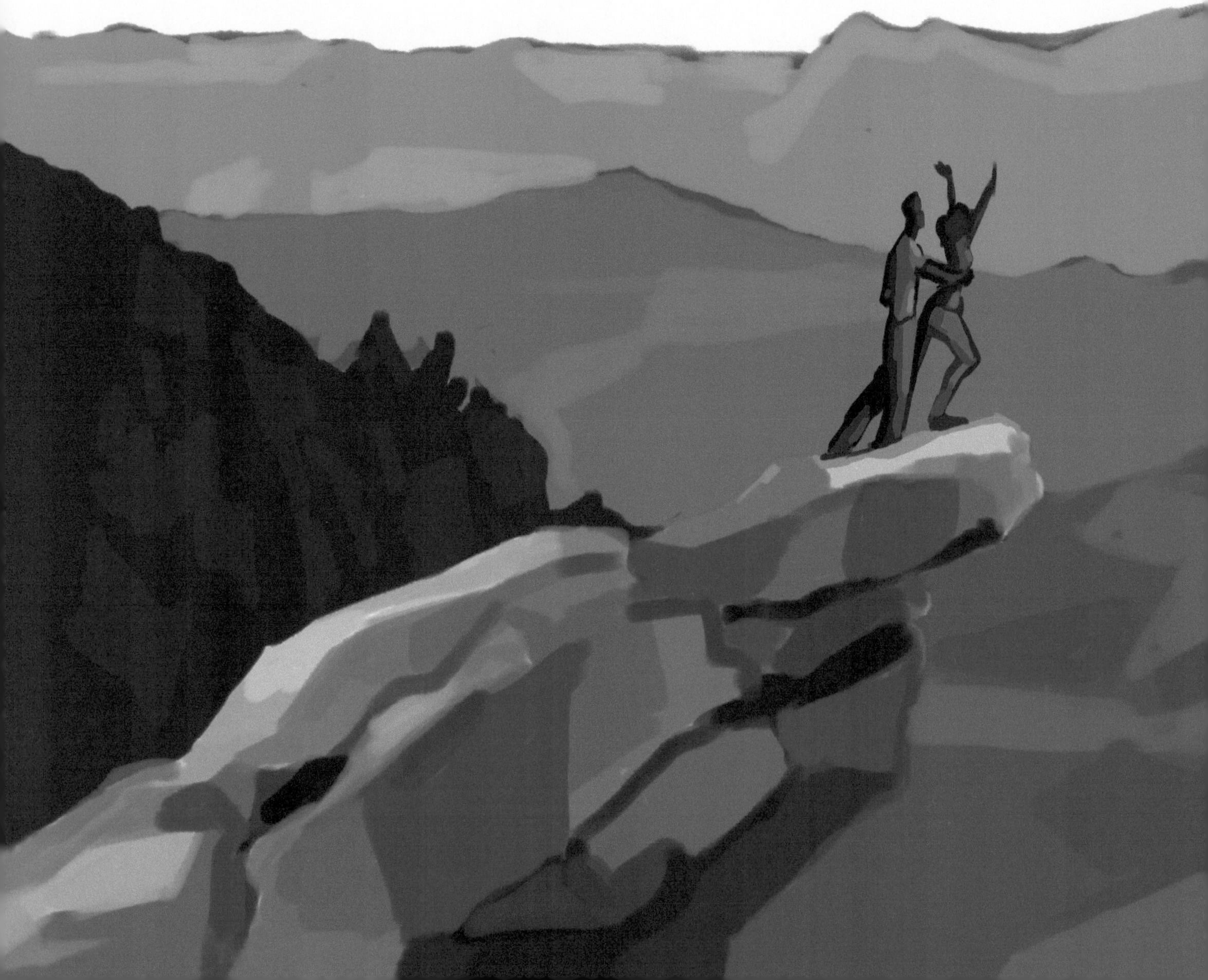

THE TYPE OF LOVE THAT WILL HAVE YOU SCREAM OUT MY NAME
SO THE WHOLE WORLD CAN HEAR

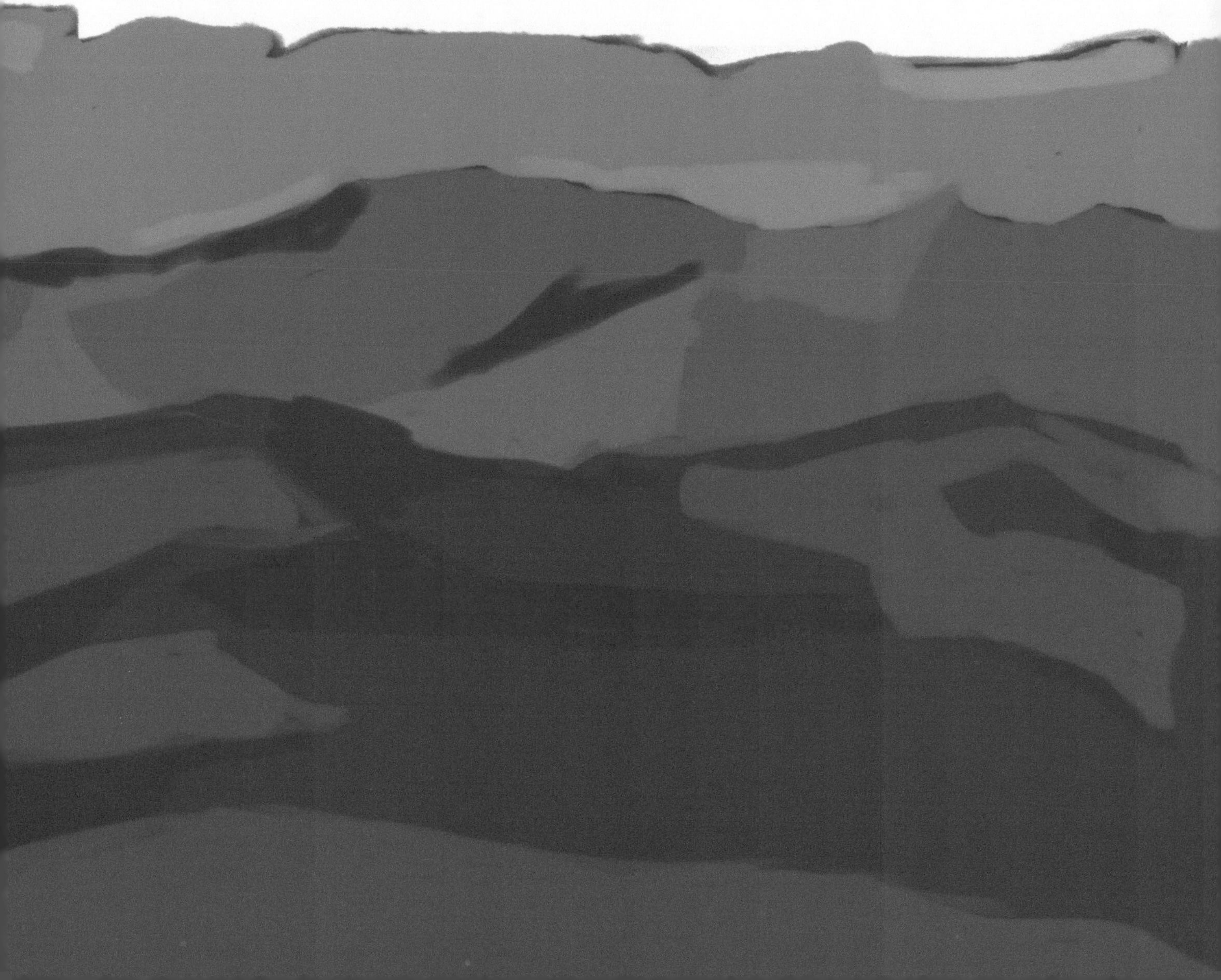

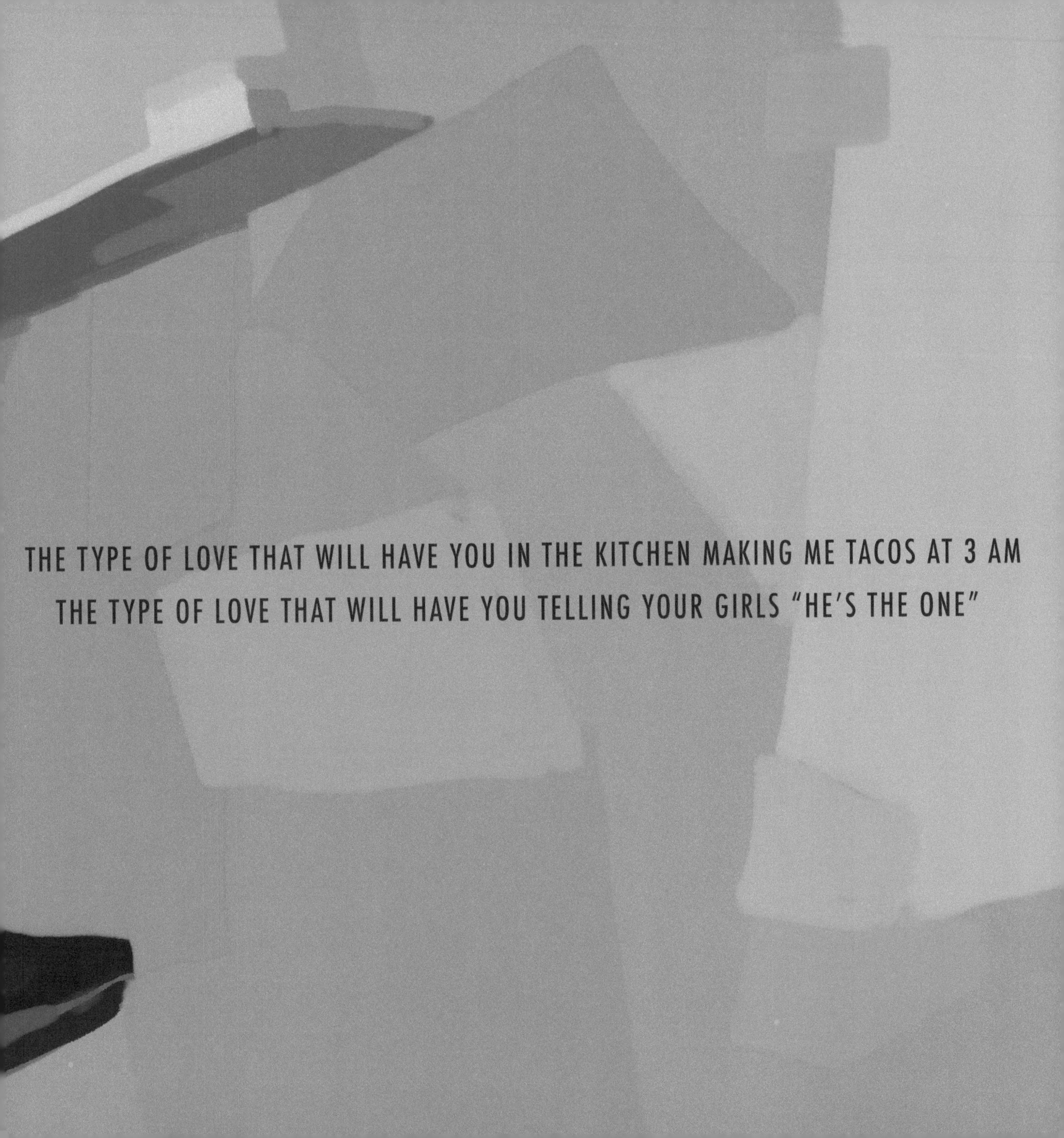

THE TYPE OF LOVE THAT WILL HAVE YOU IN THE KITCHEN MAKING ME TACOS AT 3 AM

THE TYPE OF LOVE THAT WILL HAVE YOU TELLING YOUR GIRLS "HE'S THE ONE"

THE TYPE OF LOVE THAT WILL HAVE
YOU WANTING ME TO MEET YOUR PARENTS

THE TYPE OF LOVE THAT WILL MAKE YOU WANNA CHANGE YOUR LAST NAME

THE TYPE OF LOVE THAT WILL HAVE YOU STANDING AT THE ALTER

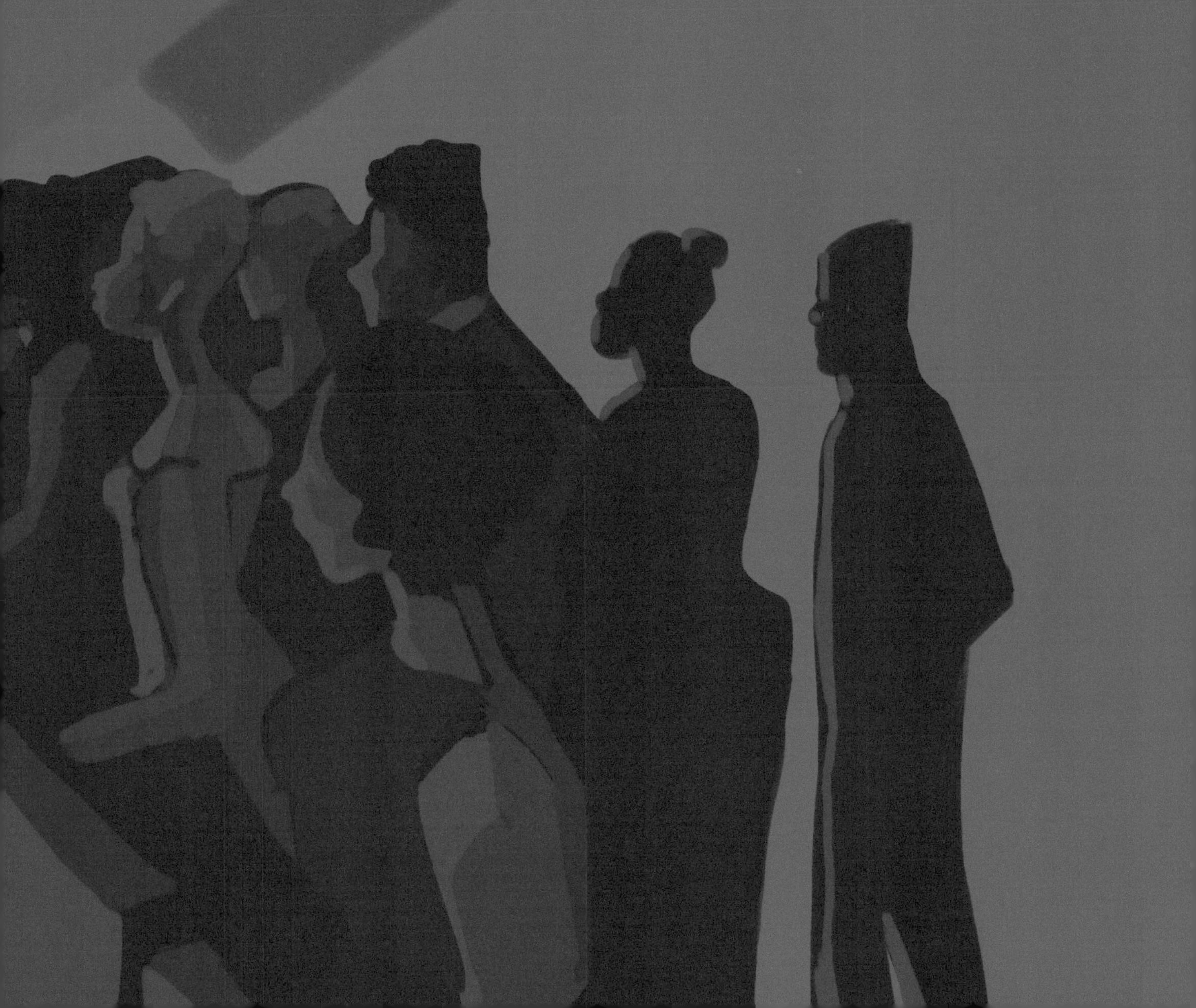

THE TYPE OF LOVE THAT WILL HAVE US GROWING
OLD TOGETHER AND RAISING A FAMILY

THE TYPE OF LOVE THAT WILL HAVE US BEING
BURIED NEXT TO EACH OTHER BECAUSE AND
I QUOTE "THATS MY LOVE"

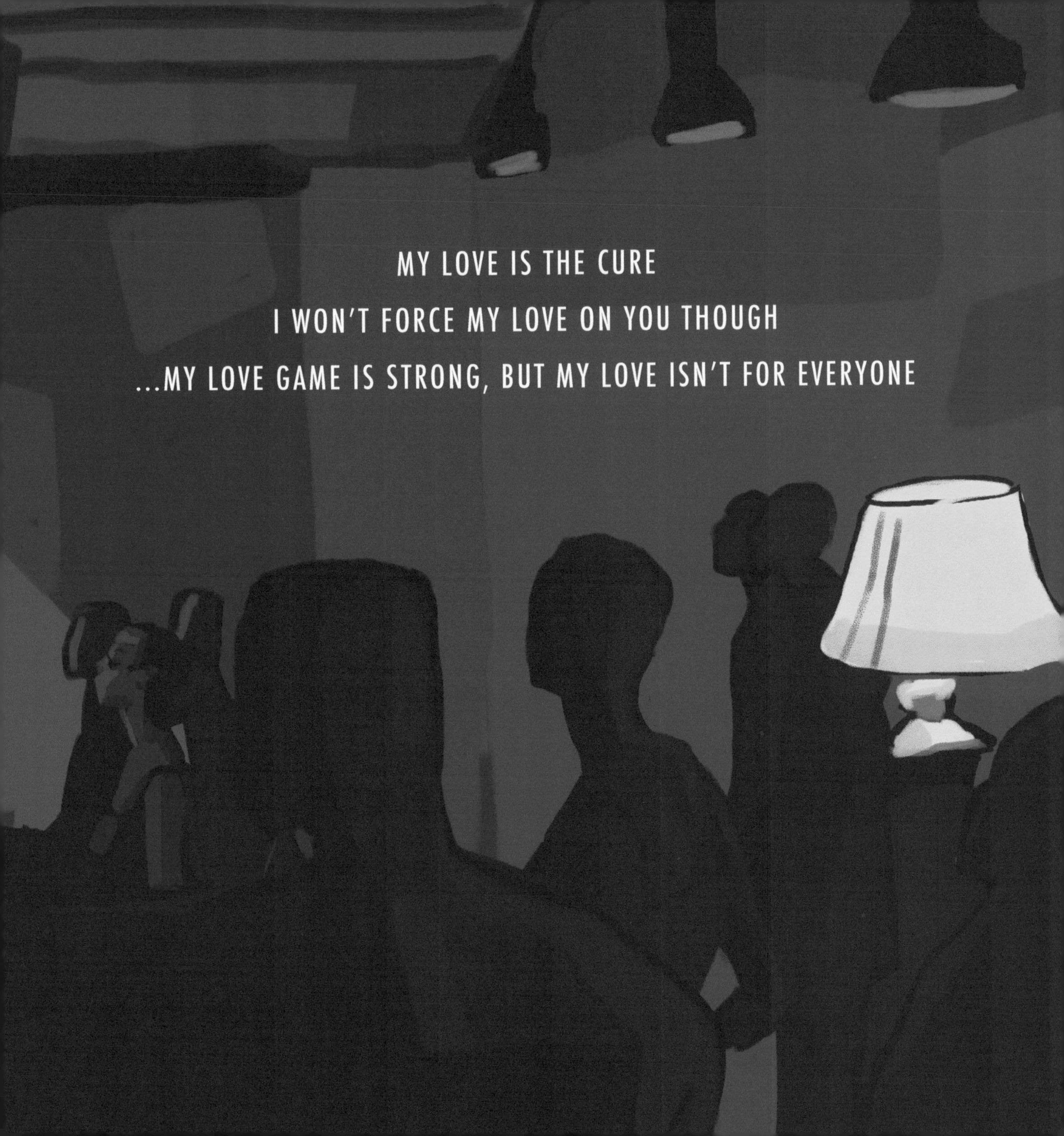

MY LOVE IS THE CURE

I WON'T FORCE MY LOVE ON YOU THOUGH

...MY LOVE GAME IS STRONG, BUT MY LOVE ISN'T FOR EVERYONE

# Eternity

It was love at first sight
like something out of a movie
The way the world seemed to stand still
as she walked in
I knew
she was my pot of gold at the end of the rainbow.

Classy, confident, intelligent
She is everything I could hope for
and more
Still my words fall on deaf ears
as she is not charmed
nor intrigued at the possibilities of us
As I gaze into her eyes,
I see her strength,
I see her pain,
yet I want to be the
one who replaces that pain
with love
and match her strength with support,
as we chase eternity
Not just another one-night stand
Where I'm left feeling empty
In a world full of uncertainty, I want more
Until then, she will remain my "what if?"

- Lightnin' Hopkins

Do you believe in love at first sight?

Flip book over to B-Side

# The Ambiguity of Love

# After Hours

"What if" isn't even an option
Love and affection for another
is not in my future
I've worked too hard to get
where I'm at in life
and now that I'm here
I'm not letting anybody derail me.

Although I am charmed by his wit
and intrigued with his allure
I can't entertain the pain of another
failed attempt at "love"
My heart and soul belong to my career
Yes, he may have the cure,
but the fix I crave isn't his heart
It's the love below
No strings attached
as I intoxicate myself
with his body.

When night turns to day
and we go our separate way
...maybe in a different time, different place
Tonight, let's enjoy the night
No regrets
Because, if it's fate
we'll find each other again someday.

- Paris Lawson

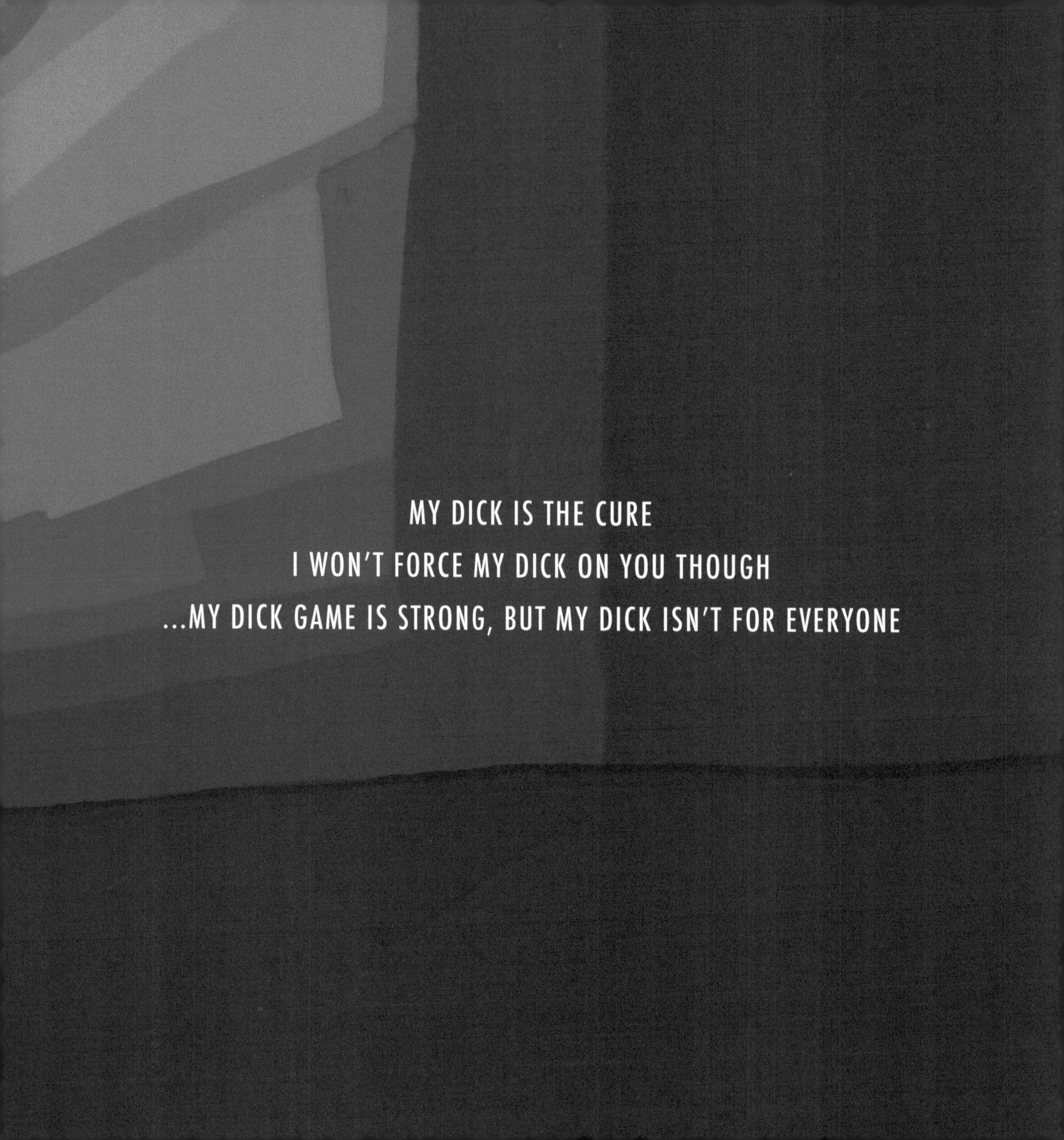
MY DICK IS THE CURE
I WON'T FORCE MY DICK ON YOU THOUGH
...MY DICK GAME IS STRONG, BUT MY DICK ISN'T FOR EVERYONE

THE TYPE OF DICK THAT WILL HAVE US BEING BURIED NEXT TO
EACH OTHER BECAUSE AND I QUOTE "THAT'S MY DICK"

PARIS
HOPKINS
THAT'S MY
LOVE →
LIGHTENIN'
HOPKINS

THE TYPE OF DICK THAT WILL HAVE US GROWING
OLD TOGETHER AND RAISING A FAMILY

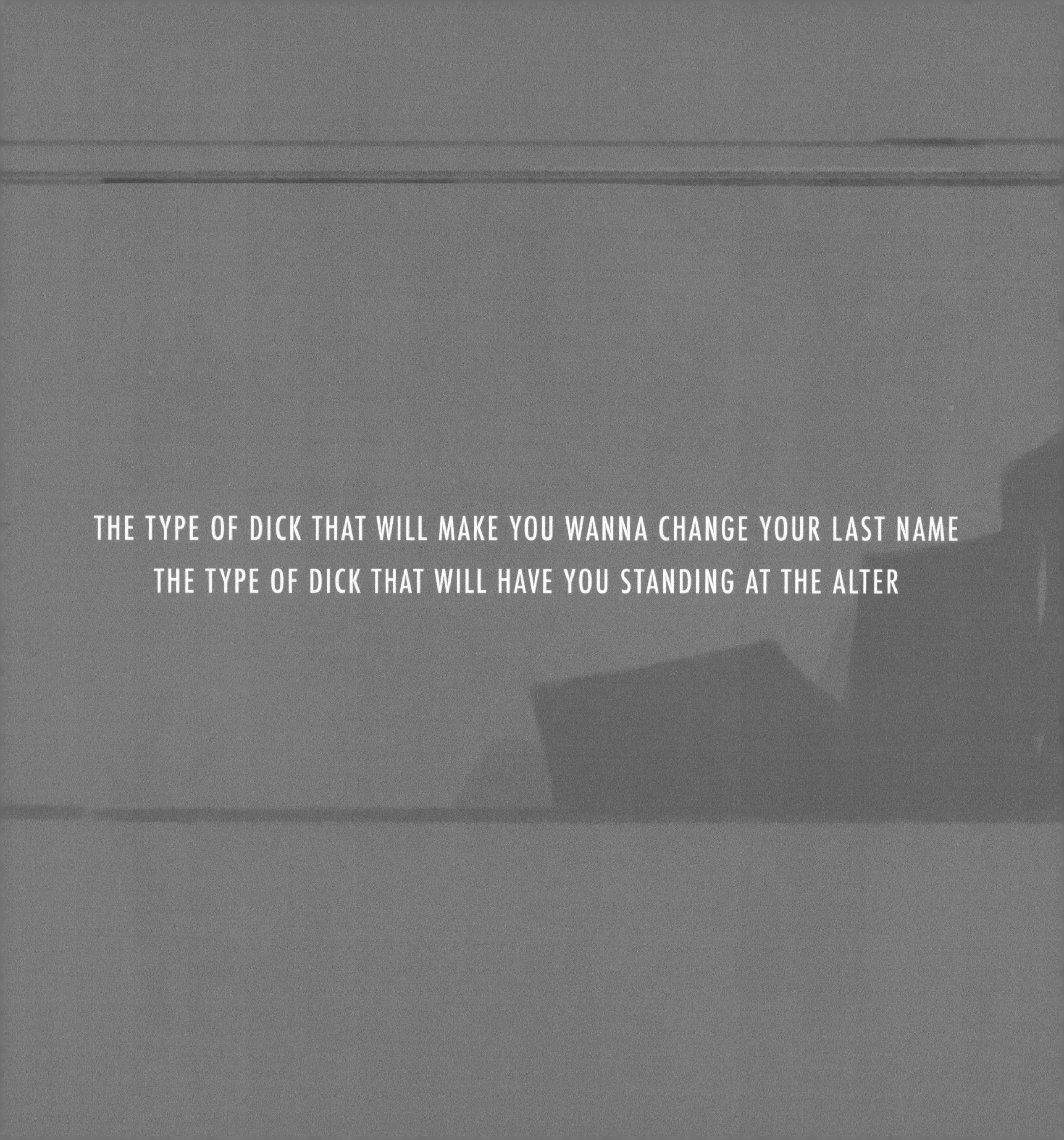
THE TYPE OF DICK THAT WILL MAKE YOU WANNA CHANGE YOUR LAST NAME
THE TYPE OF DICK THAT WILL HAVE YOU STANDING AT THE ALTER

THE TYPE OF DICK THAT WILL HAVE YOU
WANTING ME TO MEET YOUR PARENTS

THE TYPE OF DICK THAT WILL HAVE YOU IN THE KITCHEN MAKING ME TACOS AT 3 AM

THE TYPE OF DICK THAT WILL HAVE YOU TELLING YOUR GIRLS "HE'S THE ONE"

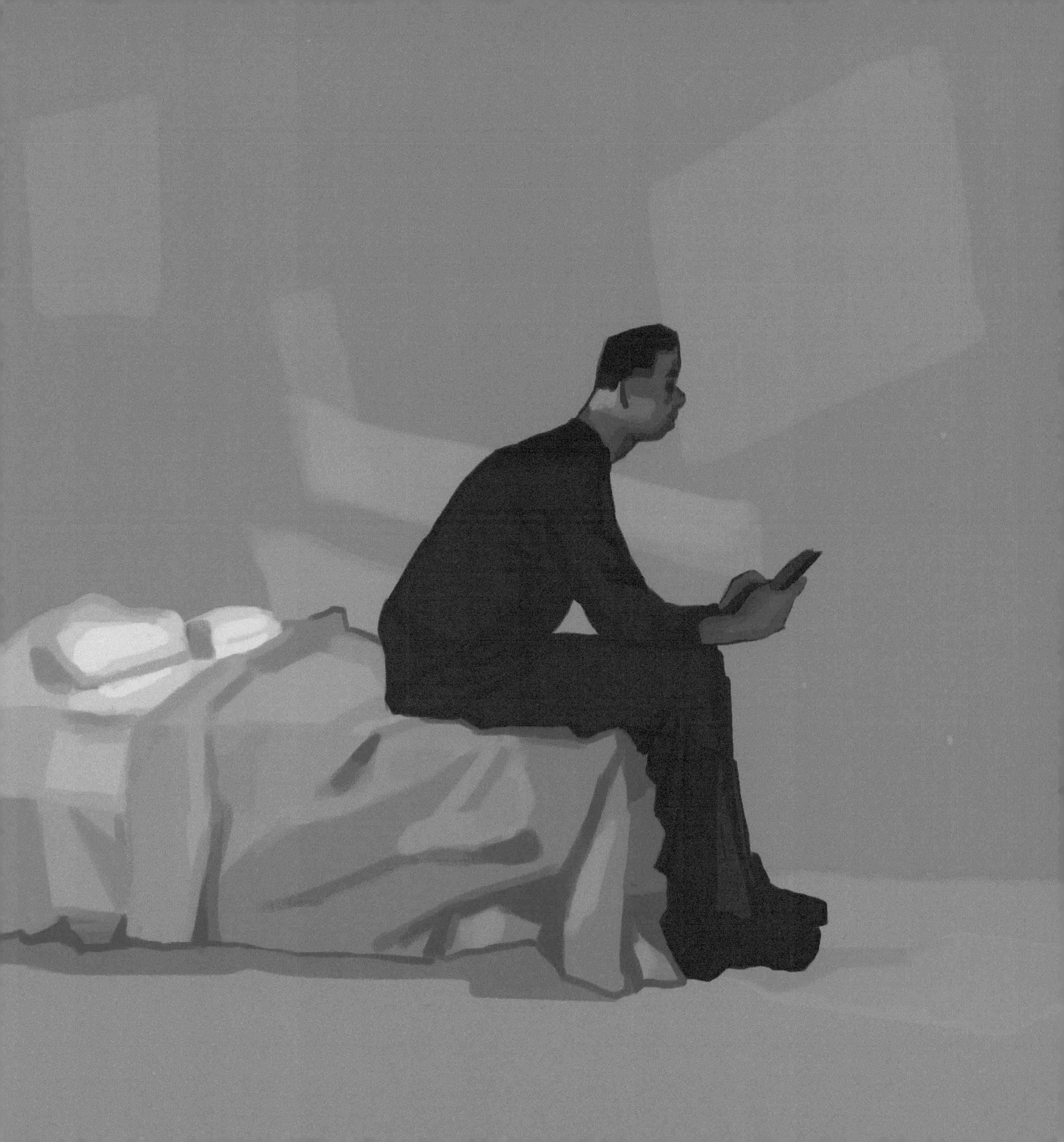

THE TYPE OF DICK THAT WILL MAKE YOU WEAK AT THE KNEES

THE TYPE OF DICK THAT WILL HAVE YOU SCREAM OUT MY NAME
SO THE WHOLE WORLD CAN HEAR

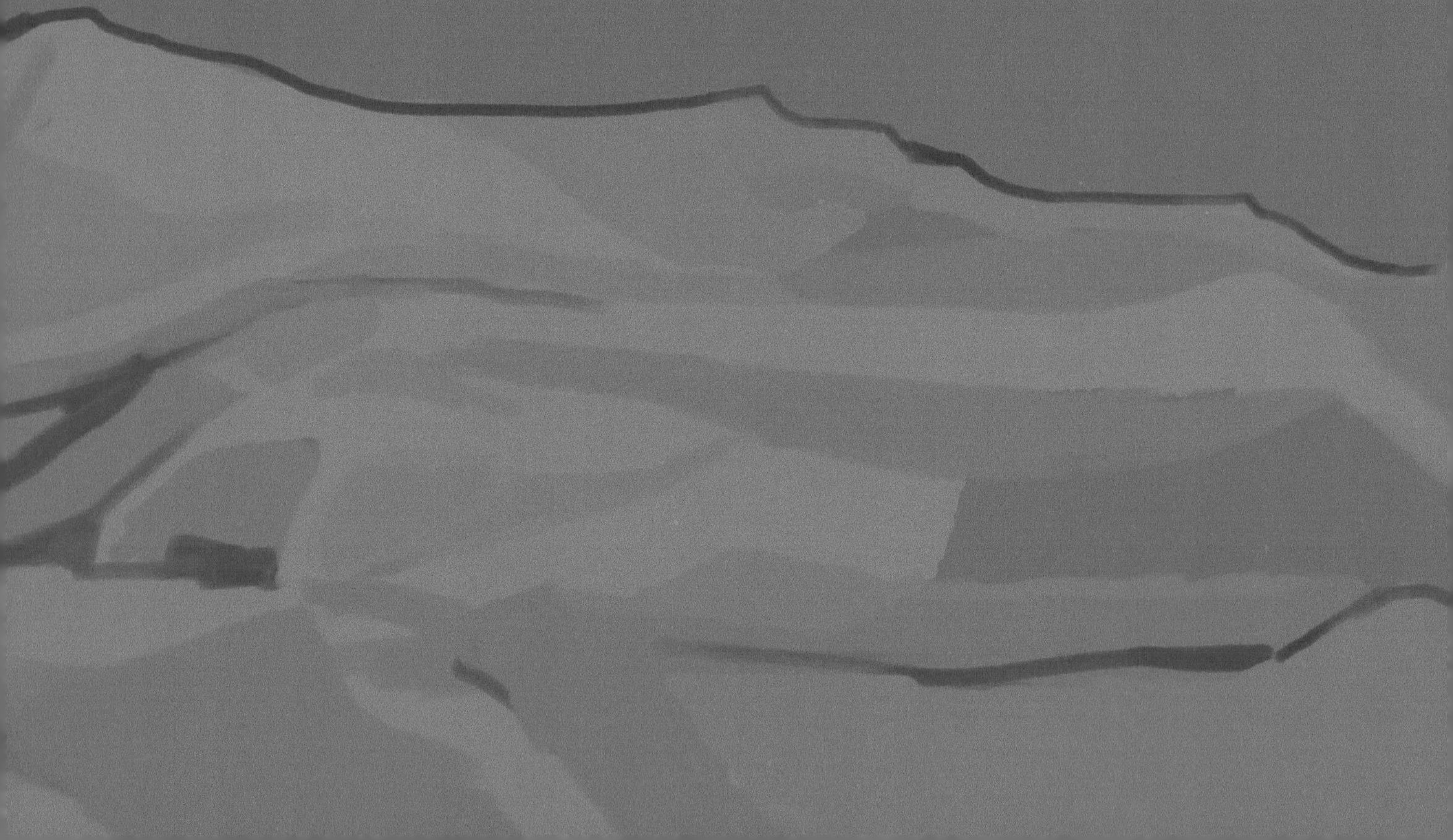

THE TYPE OF DICK YOU'VE ONLY SEEN IN MOVIES

THE TYPE OF DICK THAT WILL HAVE YOU FORGET ABOUT YOUR EXs

BUT THIS IS A ONCE IN A LIFETIME TYPE OF DICK,
THE TYPE OF DICK YOU PRAY ABOUT
THE TYPE OF DICK THAT WILL HAVE YOU FALL DEEPER THAN YOU'VE EVER FELL

MY DICK ISN'T FOR EVERYONE, BUT MY DICK GAME IS STRONG

I WON'T FORCE MY DICK ON YOU THOUGH

IF YOU DON'T WANT MY DICK I'LL WALK AWAY

# B-Side: After Hours

A Story Of Lust told from the point of view of Paris Lawson, who's tired of playing the dating game and not looking for love, but rather a good time with no strings attached. Paris is in town for the week attending a conference when she decides to step out for a drink and poetry at "The Harlem" where she runs into Hopkins with one thing on her mind: the cure to her woes.

# PREFACE

**The Cure** is a story of love vs. lust when two strangers cross paths at "The Harlem"— an upscale jazz club. Lightnin' Hopkins, a 25-year-old architect and local poet known for his sensual and romantic poetry, and Paris Lawson, a 36-year-old no-nonsense successful doctor who puts her work at the forefront, cross paths one fate filled night in search of "**the cure**."

*Dedicated to those who pushed me to write this book and helped along the way. With sincere love, this wouldn't be possible without y'all..and to those I've encountered along life's journey who inspired this book, my deepest gratitude.*

Published by 73 Homage
ISBN# 978-0-578-83695-9

73 Homage LLC
www.73homage.com
Instagram: @73homage
dontaepeoples@73homage.com

**Dontae Peoples** is a sarcastic asshole with a heart of gold who has failed at love countless times. Nevertheless, he walks a fine line between genius and insanity.

https://73homage.com

New Jersey-based Illustrator **Renee Hunt** creates character artwork in styles ranging from playful and whimsically simple to more realistic and technical images. She is a graduate from Andrews University in Michigan, where she studied oil painting, graphic design, animation, and printmaking under the best industry professionals including internationally known artist Harry Ahn. Since then, Renee has been working in New Jersey for five years. Over her career, she has created many published illustrations for a list of well-known clients. Today, Renee is engaged with illustrating for client projects in picture books, advertising, fashion, websites, and magazines.

https://reneeashleyhunt.com

# The CURE

## The Ambiguity of Love

(B-Side: After Hours)

By Dontae Peoples
Illustrated by Renee Hunt

Printed in the USA
CPSIA information can be obtained
at www.ICGtesting.com
LVHW071916011123
762817LV00009B/36